THE SECRET OF AZARATH

U.DIKSHITHA

D.HARINI

U. THILLAI

Contents

1

INTRODUCTION

Once in a beautiful village named Azarath. There was a brave girl named Kinza. She was known for her curiosity and adventures. It was December month and was freaking cold outside, so her mom told Kinza to go to the attic and get some wood.

As she went searching for wood, she found something more interesting, it was an old & dusty book in the self, she took the book and blew the dust off, It was a purple book and was known as the "Secret of Azarath" by DR.WILLIAMS.

She said to herself, "dude he is my grandpa, I need to know what is going on, wait! No, what was going on that time". Suddenly her mom called her down, she went down and her mom asked what was she doing up there for long time and were where the woods. Kinza, manages to escape from mom and went to her room, *while mom was too busy with her calls. She started reading the book as it said. "Once in a beautiful village named Azarath, with many forest, waterfalls and lion guardians. I know you reader can't believe that lion guardians were there in our village, the lion guardians took the second and third part of this book and only one part is left which is the first part which your reading now. People say that the second part is hidden behind the last waterfall known as the "WHISPERING WATERFALLS'*

' and protected by the lion guardians. Once a brave man Thomas and his teammates went searching for the book, some of the teammates returned back home

and told that most of them died in lake of Azarath most of them were drowned by the quicksand, after that we all got scared and ran to the village, after few days, we got in formation about Thomas that he have reached in the whispering waterfalls and took the second part of the book, but I have no idea where the third part is.

We started celebrating and thought Thomas would return, we waited for days and weeks, but he never returned, people say that he is dead and some people say that his Sprit is living there we still don't know what happen to Thomas and what is inside that book, do people die when there read the book? All of these questions have an answer inside that book, nobody knows.

Sincerely DR.WILLIAMS". Kinza was like, " oh my god this story, is it even real I have no idea. Omg its 12:00, I need to sleep". And she started sleeping.

THE NEXT DAY

AH! Fresh and nice Kinza said. And she started walking to her grandma's house, as she going, she asked people about the Azarath and its secrets but nobody told anything. While she was doing that she also reached her grandma's house. Dingdong the bell rang, her grandma came and opened the door and saw here little princess, grandma said," aww! My darling what are you doing here come inside.

What help my darling need?" Kinza said, "Grandma can you tell me about this book which grandpa wrote". As soon as grandma saw that book she started crying. She asked grandma why she is crying Grandma

? Grandma told that it was grandpa'sthis book in the church and once your mom took this book with herself, from that time I didn't see this book where was this book dear asked Grandma , Kinza told it was in the attic and all the things in the book. grandma said," yes dear we don't know what is in that book as soon as Thomas

died nobody had hope to take the book, and people believe that when we take all three parts and join them together the world might end". Kinza said, "I am brave enough to go and I am going to the whispering waterfalls".

Grandma said," Be careful dear there are many dangerous things around don't touch anything and don't believe anybody".

2

READY FOR AN ADVENTURE

but still, Kinza went out of the house, & asked her class d her bag with all After deciding to go on an adventure, Kinza packethe stuff, she needed and got ready for an great adventure.

NEXT DAY

Kinza woke up and got ready for the adventure, Kinza went down and told her mom that she is going to an adventure to "WHISPERING WATERFALLS". Her mom didn't want her to go,

was walking, she felt like drowning, then she saw down, it was a quicksand, she slowly opened her hand, and removed her bag, then she started moving her body up, somebody was helping her, she saw who was it,

"it was a handsome young man who was wearing a sailor teacher, Harisha about the book, and Harisha gave Kinza an old map about the adventure she is going on. Harisha,

asked if she could accompany her, as, there are many dangerous things, but Kinza rejected her offer , as she wants to go on her own. Kinza started walking towards the rainforest. After walking for three hours, she finally reached lake, then she saw sleeping crocodiles and many fishes in the lake.

She thought for a while and slowly walked over the crocodiles head, suddenly she fell over the crocodile, all the crocodiles were awake, and started chasing her, she climbed over the tree, The crocodiles got confused and went in the wrong way. She came down and started walking towards her destination.

While she costume and had blue eyes and light brown curled hair". He slowly pulled her out of the quicksand, Kinza said," Thanks , but how are you ? And what are you doing here in this dark forest? ". In reply he said, " I am Charles, I am living here with my Mom

, I was working as a sailor , later got fired as I broke a vase. If you are okay you can come and stay in my house". Kinza was okay with the offer, and went with Charles to his house, Kinza reached the house, It was a huge mushroom house which had strawberry gardens and berry sofa and chairs. Kinza got her own room, she changed her clothes and came out,

Charles made hot chocolate for them both, They sat down in the berry sofa and started talking. Charles asked, " okay why are you here and what's your name ?". Kinza said all the reason. And Charles asked that can he could also join her, Kinza without thinking anything said okay. After some time they started walking towards the Snake forest. After a long walk they reached Snake forest,

and the heard a hissing sound behind them, and they turned back they saw a big king Cobra, and they ran, so fast they were tired. And they turned back the big king Cobra wasn't there. They saw abandoned car. They searched for items they found a chips packet and a skeleton and expired items. And they saw the skeleton and got scared,

but Kinza saw a book in the skeleton's hand the book was dusty so they blew on the book's front they thought this was the book of' SECRET OF AZARATH". Kinza said, omg this is the book. They opened the book and saw a map,

Kinza said this is not the secret of Azarath, it is a map. Then Charles found a spear and some weapons like gun

& knife. They took the weapons and started walking, then they heard some water splashing nearby, they went near the bush and saw...

Whispering Falls

It was a beautiful waterfalls where there was peace and joy, birds flying all over, flowers and tree dancing for the bird's song, no noise, all peace and nice,

they went inside and started searching for the book they found it in an old skeleton holding that book, they took the second book and started reading the book, but it has a lock, to open it they need to find the riddle, It says, you buy me for eating, but you won't eat me,

who am I ? kinza was thinking for answer and told," Is it a plate?". The book opened, and they saw, azarath was the only place gold many rulers came here to rule our village but noone was like "JAKE HOOD". He came here for just ruling not for other reasons.azarath was the only place gold many rulers came here to rule our village but no one was like "JAKE HOOD".

He came here for just ruling not for other reasons, he married our girl, Chitra, they had an daughter named kiki, she was just the same as her father brave and fearless, once he an 16 young men's went for war, sadly didn't return back, chitra heartbroken told me to write all the secret of azarath, kiki his only favourite girl, was always smiling, first time crying after her birth.

From that we all were heartbroken as he did many things for us, we still can't overcome, chitra and kiki moved to another town. People say that she started a new life.From that...

Kinza was confused, Kinza saw her friend Diya and asked what was she doing here, it seems she came searching for Kinza and came here, she introduced Diya to Charles. Charles, was very happy to see Diya and Kinza together, they went to Charles's house and started discussing, Charles told," I am tired come let's sleep". They went to sleep...

NEXT DAY

They all woke up and saw something in the garden, it was an old well, a message wrote like, " come find me in this well". They went closer and saw...

The Well

*They saw something odd inside it, Kinza took a torch
and tied herself in the rope, and slowly went inside the
well, she took the torch out,*

*she saw an old chest and took it out, they came inside
the house and tried opening the chest but it had an hey
to open, Charles went inside an took an axe, and came,*

*Kinza asked what was it, Charles replied," people call
me to cut their tree for that I had an axe,". He smashed
the lock, and opened it,*

*there was a dairy, book, jewels, and a map. They
opened the book and started reading it, it said," hello I
am Lila, my mother is Kiki, yes you might know "JAKE
HOOD".*

*Yeah the great ruler who ruled Azarath the village, he
is my grandpa, I got married in 4th march 2007, and
gave birth to a beautiful son at 22nd may 2013,*

my son was not blessed his father died at a car accident, from that me and my son are living alone in this forest, I didn't tell my son his father died I told him he went to America for some work, whenever my son ask, when will papa come home,

I can't bear that pain, but, my son took care of me very well, he worked as a sailor and helped people nearby, he was very helpful boy, I love you son, I will die soon, I can feel it very well, if find's the truth now about his father, tell him I feel very sorry. I love you Charles".

Kinza was very shocked. Charles started crying, they took Charles inside the house to make him comfortable, They started opened the book it was very dusty, they wiped the dust off, they found the third part,

they all were very happy and started reading it, it was written like, " in the Azarath, in the church pull the lever to find him and the statue, help us". Kinza was like," what..."

A Statue?

They rushed to their village, went to the church, and started searching for the lever, and Charles saw the picture of Kinza's Grandpa,

by mistake he pushed the picture. The wall opened and they went inside, they saw an ancient statue, they slowly took the statue, the way started collapsing, so they took it and rushed out,

Charles started shouting so he could grab everyone's attention, everyone was seeing them they showed the statue, everyone praised the statue like god. Kinza was very happy, they started celebrating, and Kinza, Charles, Diya, became very popular from that time.

THE END

9 798899 610530